I0516914

THE SACRED LITURGY AS

A SECRET GARDEN

# THE SACRED LITURGY *as a*

## ecret

## arden

FR ARMAND DE
MALLERAY, FSSP

AROUCA
PRESS

Publication authorised by
Very Rev Fr Andrzej Komorowski,
Superior General FSSP, on 24th June 2022

Scripture quotes are from the
Douay-Rheims version.

ISBN: 978-1-990685-23-1

Arouca Press
PO Box 55003
Bridgeport PO
Waterloo, ON N2J3G0
Canada
www.aroucapress.com
Send inquiries to info@aroucapress.com

# Contents

## Foreword

# IN THE FORM
# OF A DISCLAIMER

HIS TEXT WAS written before 16<sup>th</sup> July 2021, when His Holiness Pope Francis issued the motu proprio *Traditionis Custodes*. The author meant to use literature, architecture and pastoral experience to illustrate the attachment of many laity and clergy to the *usus antiquior*. Having been appointed rector, five years earlier, to a shrine church established to serve the needs of those attached to the *usus antiquior*, and pondering on the unprecedented ordeal of the Covid-19 church closures, the author sought to share his understanding of the signs of the times without entering here into theological arguments.

Similarly, fifty years earlier, men and women of culture, some Catholic, some Protestant, some of other religions, had appealed for the preservation of the traditional Roman liturgy which, *"in its magnificent Latin text, has also inspired a host of priceless achievements in the arts — not only mystical works, but works by poets, philosophers, musicians, architects, painters and sculptors in all countries and epochs. Thus, it belongs to universal culture."* Pope Paul VI had granted their request in what became known as the *Agatha Christie Indult*.[1]

The present pamphlet was planned for release as a special edition of the quarterly magazine *Dowry* celebrating its fiftieth issue in the summer 2021. Subsequently, *Traditionis Custodes* surprised the Church, as expressed in many reactions at the highest level. The author first thought it preferable to postpone publishing an essay on such a volatile topic, lest it were misinterpreted as polemical. On reflection, since cultural forms and pastoral anecdotes are used instead of liturgical and theological demonstrations, submitting the text as a respectful and dispassionate *Apologia*

---

1   Mgr. Annibale Bugnini, of the Sacred Congregation for Divine Worship, conveyed the decision officially to Cardinal Heenan of Westminster on 5th November 1971. Cf. https://lms.org.uk/1971-english-indult-recollection.

*pro Missa dilecta*[2] was deemed acceptable.[3] Since it had been written prior to His Holiness' motu proprio, it offered a genuine perspective on the *usus antiquior* as experienced by a local community in good standing, with no other agenda than growth in holiness, by the grace of God and with the blessing of Holy Church.

Since September 2021 when this text was published in the magazine *Dowry*, Pope Francis has confirmed by decree[4] dated 11th February 2022 the liturgical identity of the author's Fraternity. This latest approval of the traditional Roman liturgy by the Vicar of Christ made the release of the text as a book even more opportune to foster appreciation of the *usus antiquior* by a wider audience.

*Fr Armand de Malleray, FSSP*
Feast of St Bede the Venerable,
27th May 2022,
at St Mary's Shrine, Warrington

---

2   In the spirit of St. John-Henry Newman's 1864 *Apologia Pro Vita Sua.*
3   Permission to publish was received on 3rd September 2021.
4   Cf. www.fssp.org/en/decree-of-pope-francis-confirming-the-use-of-the-1962-liturgical-books/

# *Introduction*

## FICTION AND REALITY

**N**OT ONLY CHILdren but adults too like stories. Whether watched on a screen, listened to as audio books or merely read as texts, tales are a pleasant way of considering important truths. Our Lord Jesus himself used fiction when teaching the crowds in parables. In his *Parable of the Sower*, he even provided the interpretation. Similarly, this pamphlet will first examine a short novel in order to draw from it some reflections on the needs of the Church following the 2020 global pandemic. Those refer not to England only, but to wherever Catholicism, once strong, is now in decline. Rather than presenting readers with solutions, this little essay invites them

1

into a garden. Along its lush flower beds we hope to make happy encounters, or even life-changing ones as did St Mary Magdalene in a certain garden on Easter morning. Let us now explain our scope more in details.

One of the most successful books of children's literature, *The Secret Garden*[1] (1911) by English novelist Frances Hodgson Burnett,[2] was adapted as a film again last year,[3] starring Oscar winner Colin Firth. Burnett's novel describes the transformation of sour orphaned Mary Lennox into a lovable companion after she has been sent back from India to England at the turn of the twentieth century. The young girl's improvement is prompted by the discovery of an enclosed garden in Misselthwaite Manor, her uncle's estate in Yorkshire. Inspired and encouraged by her visits into the secret garden, Mary manages to bring her sickly cousin Colin back to health. The children eventually save even Uncle Archibald Craven, Colin's widowed father, from his depressive mourning.

---

1   The full text of the novel is accessible online on https://www.gutenberg.org/files/17396/17396-h/17396-h.htm.
2   She had previously published two successful children's novels: *Little Lord Fauntleroy* (1885–1886) and *A Little Princess* (1905).
3   We recommend watching the 1993 film, truer to the book than the latest 2020 one.

Fountains Abbey in Yorkshire, a Cistercian architectural jewel destroyed by Henry VIII, was selected for the 2020 film adaptation as had already been the case for the 1993 film. This choice is surprising since no mention is made in the story of monastic ruins at Misselthwaite Manor, unlike in *The Red Moon of Meru* (1927), a brilliant short-story by G. K. Chesterton (1874–1936) about the theft of an Indian ruby at the Anglican stately home of "Mallowood Abbey." In the very last lines of his story, Chesterton's ironical denunciation of the theft of Catholic estates by Anglican opportunists of old is unexpectedly pointed and literarily brilliant:

> 'Other English gentlemen have stolen before now, and been covered by legal and political protection; and the West also has its own way of covering theft with sophistry. After all, the ruby is not the only kind of valuable stone in the world that has changed owners; it is true of other precious stones; often carved like cameos and coloured like flowers.' The other looked at him inquiringly; and the priest's finger was pointed to the Gothic outline of the great Abbey. 'A great graven stone,' he said, 'and that was also stolen.'

Admittedly, Frances Hodgson Burnett's novel entails no such Catholic stance. However, we find the coincidental location of the two film adaptations at Fountains Abbey suggestive. We propose to use it as a key to a symbolic reading of *The Secret Garden*, envisaged as a tale about pre-Anglican England and about the Church traditions, little accessed in the postconciliar era and rediscovered by many during and after the Covid-19 crisis.

Novelist Frances Hodgson Burnett (1849–1924) was born in Manchester one year before the reestablishment of the Catholic hierarchy in England (promulgated by Pope Pius IX in his bull *Universalis Ecclesiae* of 29th September 1850). The girl grew up in an average lower-middle-class Anglican family. She later moved to America where she was married, but still spent time in England thereafter. While there is no evidence that she was interested in Catholicism, its rebirth would surely not have escaped her keen intellect. Fiction writers draw from actual events, refashioned and combined to create original situations. Burnett's biographers could tell us whether or not she ever meant to use England's pre-Anglican religious identity in her novels. For our purpose, the comparatively short text of her *Secret Garden* (81,000 words in 27 chapters) yields various clues which, for traditional Catholics in England, evoke a longing for pre-Reformation Merry England. For her writings Burnett drew abundantly from her own experiences, either painful ones (leaving England, losing her son), or happy ones (an actual robin showed her the entrance into her beloved garden at Great Maytham Hall). In addition, she was by no means a Christian apologist, leaning instead toward Spiritualism. Religious innuendoes in *The Secret Garden* point towards what we would nowadays call New Age, rather than toward Christianity (unless subconsciously). Therefore, leaving aside the novelist's psyche and her authorial motivations, we offer this personal interpretation as an historical exercise and as a pious entertainment to illustrate the crucial topic of Catholic traditions nearly lost and gradually rediscovered.

## Part One

---

# PRESENTATION
# OF THE NOVEL
# *THE SECRET GARDEN*

### MOTHERLESS

HE STORY BEGINS in colonial India where Mary's mother embodies beautiful but unmotherly femininity. The little girl behaves tyrannically because she is not loved. An outbreak of cholera soon makes her an orphan and causes her repatriation to England, her paradoxically unknown motherland across the oceans. The first chapter is interestingly titled *There is no one left*. All either have been killed by the disease or have fled it. Little Mary was simply forgotten. Thus, the story starts with a catastrophe. We like to see it as a domestic transposition of Henry VIII's *Act of Supremacy* (1534). Young Mary stands for the soul of England as a once Catholic nation, depopulated of Catholic folk. This took place across Our Lady's Dowry under the Tudor persecution, when opposition to King Henry from clergy, religious and the laity was horribly crushed, leading most of the population and hierarchy to embrace the new made-up religion. Over the following three centuries, England became more powerful, richer and culturally influent. In the novel, Mary's mother would fit well as a symbol of (post-)Victorian Britain: proud, attractive, imposing, but lacking that inner life of the soul.

## TWO MARY-LIKE MOTHERS

In contrast, the country woman Susan Sowerby is the actual embodiment of motherhood in the story. Mrs Sowerby is the loving mother of twelve children, including Mary's protectress Martha, and Mary's playmate Dickon. Because Martha only ever refers to her as *Mother*, orphaned Mary imitates her, thus gaining a quasi foster-mother. To an Anglican novelist like Burnett, Industrial Revolution Manchester provided far too many examples of exhausted Irish immigrant mothers, for whom motherhood appeared like a fate and their many children as a cause of social and spiritual wretchedness. Against such a background, one could have expected anti-Catholic prejudice in the portraying of a low-income mother of a large family.[1] On the contrary, Mrs Sowerby is depicted as utterly lovable, glorious and benevolent despite having a dozen children, no wealth and a husband never mentioned. Entailing the word "sower", her surname reflects her blessed fecundity, an embodiment of the natural growth felicitously at work in the garden. It is not enough to identify her as a Catholic, but it certainly confirms her Marian features such as her *long blue cloak* resembling a vestment. Further, her first "apparition" in the novel — notably in the secret garden itself, rather than at the hall or in the village — reads precisely as a supernatural manifestation, perhaps influenced by what Burnett might have read about the apparitions of the Virgin Mary in Lourdes (1858). With theological timeliness, the Mary-like

---

1 Another Mancunian female novelist, Elizabeth Gaskell (1810–1865), had written about the working class in Manchester, while a third contemporary woman from the same area, Elizabeth Prout (1820–1864; declared Venerable by Pope Francis on 21st January 2021) was dubbed by the BBC "the Mother Teresa of Manchester" in recognition of her heroic work among the thousands of destitute in the industrial slums, especially Catholic immigrants fleeing the Irish potato famine. What an interesting conversation might have taken place among such outstanding women, had they met.

vision follows the children's confident invoking of the Blessed Trinity:

> Praise Father, Son, and Holy Ghost. Amen…
> The door in the ivied wall had been pushed
> gently open and a woman had entered. She
> had come in with the last line of their song
> and she had stood still listening and looking
> at them. With the ivy behind her, the sun-
> light drifting through the trees and dappling
> her long blue cloak, and her nice fresh face
> smiling across the greenery she was rather
> like a softly coloured illustration in one of
> Colin's books. She had wonderful affection-
> ate eyes which seemed to take everything
> in — all of them, even Ben Weatherstaff and
> the 'creatures' and every flower that was in
> bloom. Unexpectedly as she had appeared,
> not one of them felt that she was an intruder
> at all. Dickon's eyes lighted like lamps. 'It's
> mother — that's who it is!'

Secondly, the dead mother of Colin is, like Our Lady in recusant England, altogether hidden and present, as symbolised in the quasi-liturgical display of her portrait in the bedroom of her crippled son (Chapter 13):

> 'I am going to let you look at something,'
> he said. 'Do you see that rose-colored
> silk curtain hanging on the wall over the
> mantel-piece?'
> Mary had not noticed it before, but she
> looked up and saw it. It was a curtain of

soft silk hanging over what seemed to be some picture.

'Yes,' she answered.

'There is a cord hanging from it,' said Colin. 'Go and pull it.'

Mary got up, much mystified, and found the cord. When she pulled it the silk curtain ran back on rings and when it ran back it uncovered a picture. It was the picture of a girl with a laughing face. She had bright hair tied up with a blue ribbon and her gay, lovely eyes were exactly like Colin's unhappy ones, agate gray and looking twice as big as they really were because of the black lashes all round them.

'She is my mother,' said Colin complainingly. 'I don't see why she died. Sometimes I hate her for doing it.'

'How queer!' said Mary.

'If she had lived I believe I should not have been ill always,' he grumbled. 'I dare say I should have lived, too. And my father would not have hated to look at me.'

This fictional scene is reminiscent of the sacred depictions of the Mother of God hidden away in some secret closets in recusant halls across England under Penal Times, and unveiled only after the Crown commissioners have searched the house in vain. Colin's sorrow would ring no less true if spoken by an Anglican squire standing under the lonely great arch of Walsingham Priory. It would express very well the regrets of Anglicans having conformed to Protestantism out of fear or weariness, but in their hearts missing the public worship, processions, banners, votive candles and pilgrimages to shrines of "Our Lady Mary."[2]

## WHO IS *MISTRESS MARY*?

"Mistress Mary" is how the main character, young orphan Mary Lennox, is referred to in the book. This does not occur once or twice by way of introduction, or merely to express deference when staff address her, but all along the narrative as well, 51 times in total. The novelist clearly saw it as meaningful. *Mistress Mary* actually was the working title of the book. "Mistress Mary" is meant as a quote of the famous English nursery rhyme:

> Mistress Mary, quite contrary,
> How does your garden grow?
> With silver bells, and cockle shells,
> And marigolds all in a row.

To tease sulky Mary, the vicar's son Basil started calling the young girl "Mistress Mary, quite contrary," singing the whole rhyme in childish derision of her. The oldest printed version of *Mistress Mary Quite Contrary* was

---

2   In *The Stripping of the Altars* (1992, Yale University), Eamon Duffy demonstrated the popular support for Catholic devotional life throughout England (from 1400 to 1580) up to and during the Tudor Protestantisation.

published in *Tommy Thumb's Pretty Songbook* in 1744. It is considered to be the first anthology of English nursery rhymes ever published.[3] Its late dating rules out neither interpretation of the rhyme, whether pro- or anti-Catholic. What online presentations of the rhyme agree upon is, hidden under the bucolic garden depiction, its likely reference to Queen Mary Tudor. Through the innocent rhyme, the Catholic daughter of Henry VIII would either be hailed by Catholics as a champion of the Old Faith restored, or vilified by Protestants as a bloody oppressor. Every word in the short poem takes a pious or bigoted meaning according to the perspective chosen. Burnet betrays no anti-Catholic sentiment in her use of the rhyme, which she effectively sets as the core of the plot. The short text of *Mistress Mary, Quite Contrary* functions in the composition of the book like a seed: it foretells the blessed germination unfolding throughout *The Secret Garden*. Rather than mock Catholic rule back in history, *Mistress Mary, Quite Contrary* heralds a spiritual awakening. In connection with the Mary-like role of Susan[4] Sowerby in the

---

3   According to https://poemanalysis.com/nursery
-rhyme/mary-mary-quite-contrary/.
4   Without starting an exegesis of *The Secret Garden*, one may note in passing that Susan bears the name of a holy woman ("Susanna"), virtuous and falsely accused by lustful men in her very garden where she would have

novel, it would not be out of place to read the frequent mention of young Mary Lennox as "Mistress Mary" as a hint to the loving Mother of God, true Mistress of England her Dowry, the Blessed Virgin Mary.

MARY'S GARDEN

In that perspective, the entire book lends itself to an interpretation of the children's garden as an education of the soul in grace, conducted by the invisible Mother. If every flower represents a virtue, and since Our Lady was endowed with all of them as befitting the Mother of God, then the garden itself symbolises the presence and the very person of the Blessed Virgin Mary.

> [Dickon] threw himself upon his knees and Mary went down beside him. They had come upon a whole clump of crocuses burst into purple and orange and gold. Mary bent her face down and kissed and kissed them. 'You never kiss a person in that way,' she said when she lifted her head. 'Flowers are so different.' He looked puzzled but smiled. 'Eh!' he said, 'I've kissed mother many a time that way when I come in from th' moor after a day's roamin' an' she stood there at th' door in th' sun, lookin' so glad an' comfortable.'

died, had it not been for young Daniel's prophetic intervention (cf. Book of Daniel 13).

Dickon's mother, Susan Sowerby, bears witness to the presence of unseen motherhood in the garden, bestowing tenderness upon Master Colin and Mistress Mary as if they were her children too:

> All at once Susan Sowerby bent down and drew [Colin] with her warm arms close against the bosom under the blue cloak — as if he had been Dickon's brother. The quick mist swept over her eyes. 'Eh! dear lad!' she said. 'Thy own mother's in this 'ere very garden, I do believe. She couldna' keep out of it.'

Furthermore, in response to the prayer of his abandoned son Colin, Archibald Craven is healed from his depression through a dream when his late wife discloses to him where she awaits him:

> 'Lilias! Lilias!' he answered. 'Lilias! where are you?' 'In the garden,' it came back like a sound from a golden flute. 'In the garden!'

The name of the deceased mother — yet alive in spirit — echoes the symbolic name traditionally associated with Our Lady, after the *Song of Solomon* (2:1):

> I am ... a lily of the valleys.

The same inspired text further calls the bride,

A garden enclosed is my sister, my spouse; a garden enclosed, a fountain sealed up (4:12).

Or in Latin:

*Hortus conclusus soror mea, sponsa, hortus conclusus, fons signatus.*

Catholic Tradition subsequently applied this description to Our Blessed Lady, the New Eve, in relation to the New Adam Our Lord Jesus. Thus, the secret garden is plausibly seen as Our Lady herself. Marian faith and devotion within Holy Church constitute the frame appointed by God for souls to heal and grow, if only they will find access to such a "garden."

What a contrast with the garden depicted in another children's book, *Alice in Wonderland* (1865), by a contemporary of Frances Hodgson Burnett (born like her in North West England), Charles Dodgson, also known as Lewis Carroll (1832–1898). Unlike young Mary's, Alice's garden is a place haunted by grotesque, weird and even homicidal characters. Carroll's tyrannical "Queen of Hearts" hates white roses and her recurrent utterance about her subjects is, "Off with their heads!" But in *The Secret Garden*, Our Blessed Lady invisibly reigns and soothes as the true Queen and Mother of all pure and humble hearts, granting them peace, tenderness and protection.[5]

---

5   We share below the presentation of the book *A*

THE ELUSIVE *MISSEL*

The peculiar name chosen for the Yorkshire estate where the action takes place is *Misselthwaite Manor*. No such toponym shows on

---

*Garden for Our Lady, Reviving the ancient tradition of Mary Gardens* by Felicity Surridge, illustrated by Malcolm Surridge, Gracewing, England.

Plants and flowers associated with the Blessed Virgin Mary originated with the early Church Fathers, who saw her prefigured in passages from the Old Testament containing nature imagery, such as: "I am a rose of Sharon, a lily of the valley" (Canticles 2:1).

St Benedict (AD 480–550) was the first recorded saint to create a garden at his monastery, as a place for prayer and contemplation. His was a rose garden or "rosary". It was St Fiacre (an Irish Saint) in 670, however, who became the first to plant a garden in honour of Our Lady, using those flowers which bore her name.

This idea quickly spread throughout Ireland and England, with many "Mary Gardens" being created to honour our Lady. These were places often close to a church, where people could go to spend quiet time in prayer with our Lady. They were often enclosed gardens with a simple statue of the Blessed Virgin, surrounded by the shrubs and flowers which had been named after her.

In Britain, so many plants originally had Marian names and meanings, that it was actually possible to have themed "Mary Garden" based around particular attributes of Our Lady and her life — a garden specifically devoted to her virtues, or her earthly life, or her joys and sorrows for example. Mary Gardens flourished right up to the time of the Reformation.

The Marian names and symbolism of the flowers of pre-Reformation England were largely omitted from English herbals and gardening books

Google Maps, but it occurs 35 times in the novel. "Thwaite" means "a piece of wild land cleared or reclaimed for cultivation." This sounds like an extended garden. Thwaite is also the name of the local village. The word *"missel"* is only known in English in connection with "thrush", a "mistle thrush" being a small to medium-sized ground living bird, supposedly feeding on mistletoe. But Burnett uses the rare spelling *"missel,"* from the Old English *"mis-tel"*, "basil, mistletoe." This may be immaterial. Musing further, though, we recall that with her husband, she lived two years in Catholic Paris, where their son Vivian was born in 1876. (In *The Secret Garden*, she quotes in French the title of the fairy tale *Riquet à la Houppe*.) It is likely that she would have known the meaning of the French word *"missel,"* namely, a book to follow or offer the Holy Sacrifice of the Mass, hence our English equivalent *"missal"* (from the final words of Holy Mass: "Ite, *missa* est.") Burnet uses the same word in connection with the land around the house: *"We've got to drive five miles across Missel Moor before we get to the Manor."* As the garden becomes a sanctuary to

produced in the 16th century. In a short space of time, 800 years of floral Marian connections and symbolism had disappeared from our gardens and countryside along with the monasteries and shrines…

(Cf. http://www.gracewing.co.uk/page149.html)

young Mary, she is compared with the bird: *"'If tha' was a missel thrush an' showed me where thy nest was, does tha' think I'd tell anyone? Not me,' he said. 'Tha' art as safe as a missel thrush.'"* What did Burnett intend "missel" to evoke? Was it a plant, "mistletoe," connoting rebirth and the ultimate triumph of life since mistletoe blossoms even in frozen winter; or a bird, namely the "missel thrush"? Moors are devoid of trees needed for mistletoe to grow. It must therefore be the bird. However, whereas the estate is likely to have been named after the moor where such birds must have dwelt in large numbers, surprisingly, no living missel thrush is ever seen in the story. The only one depicted is merely drawn on paper by Mary's playmate, the country boy Dickon. Despite being ink on paper, that *missel* is no altar *missal*, just a little sketch of a bird. In our Catholic recusant hermeneutic of *The Secret Garden*, *"Misselthwaite"* could sound like a poignant codename for *"moor-of-altar-missals"* ("popish" missals stolen, burnt, hidden or found again). Less cryptically, we can state that the unusual name evokes life natural and supernatural, altogether familiar, mysterious and sacred. In 1900, Thomas Hardy's poem *The Darkling Thrush* contrasted the bleak spirit of modern age with the religious hope expressed by a little bird *"in a full-hearted evensong / Of joy illimited"* in defiance of wintery gloom. Burnett's "missel" performs a similar function.

## ROBIN REDBREAST OF *MISSELTHWAITE MANOR*

If no missel thrush is seen flying above Misselthwaite, yet a very much alive *robin* is mentioned no less than 113 times in the book. Described as a lovable creature, the bird seems endowed with consciousness. The robin is explicitly connected with *Missel Moor* by the gardener: *"th' finest cock robin on Missel Moor."*[6] It is he who guides Mary towards the hole where the key to the secret garden lay concealed. He interacts with the children and with the gardener in many other ways. Christian stories from medieval times have connected the redbreast robin with Christ, either in his Nativity (the bird's breast turned red when he tried to fan the dying fire to keep warm the newborn Child) or in his Death. The latter symbolic association was expounded by Selma Lägerlof (1858–1940), the celebrated Swedish author of children's book, whose series of *Christ Legends*, one of which is titled *Robin Redbreast*,[7] was published in English in New York in 1908 just

---

6   The famous English nursery rhyme *Who Killed Cock Robin* has a mistle thrush sing for the dead robin: "Who'll sing a psalm? I, said the Thrush, as she sat on a bush, I'll sing a psalm."
7   Full text online on https://www.gutenberg.org/files/44818/44818-h/44818-h.htm.

when Burnett had moved there permanently. The following year, Lägerlof became the first woman awarded the Nobel Prize of Literature. It is very probable that Burnett would have read the latest production of a celebrated fellow female author of children's literature, the very same year when she was writing *The Secret Garden* (published as a series from 1910 to 1911 before its release as a book). Lägerlof wrote:

"little by little [the robin] gained courage, flew close to [Jesus], and drew with his little bill a thorn that had become imbedded in the brow of the Crucified One. And as he did this there fell on his breast a drop of blood from the face of the Crucified One;—it spread quickly and floated out and coloured all the little fine breast feathers."[8]

---

8   Quote continued:

Then the Crucified One opened his lips and whispered to the bird: "Because of thy compassion, thou hast won all that thy kind have been striving after, ever since the world was created."

As soon as the bird had returned to his nest his young ones cried to him: "Thy breast is red! Thy breast feathers are redder than the roses!"

"It is only a drop of blood from the poor man's forehead," said the bird; "it will vanish as soon as I bathe in a pool or a clear well."

But no matter how much the little bird bathed, the red colour did not vanish — and when his little young ones grew up, the blood-red colour shone also on their breast feathers, just as it shines on every Robin Redbreast's throat and breast until this very day.

Before dying a Catholic convert in Paris, Oscar Wilde (1854–1900), had also associated a kind-hearted bird and a bloody sacrifice of love in *The Nightingale and the Rose*, included in his 1888 volume of children's literature *The Happy Prince and Other Tales*. It is likely that Burnett would have read that book as well. Although not a figure of Christ, the redbreast robin in *The Secret Garden* is connected with the sacred mystery of life concealed in the walled garden.

## THE KEY

The word "key" occurs 34 times in the novel. Every time (but one) it refers to the key to the secret garden. Uncle Archibald Craven had buried it into the ground in desperation after the accidental death of his beloved wife Lilias, killed by a falling branch. Because she loved the garden so much, Archibald forbade access to it forever. The robin showed Mary where to find the key. The key is an eminently symbolic item in literature. Our Lord himself used the word in that way when commissioning the Apostle St Peter as his first Vicar, to whom he would entrust the keys of his kingdom, so that whatsoever Peter (and his successors) would bind on earth would be bound in heaven, and whatsoever he would loose on earth would be loosed in heaven.[9] In the novel, the key

---

9   Cf. Matthew 18:18.

is plainly what secures access to the garden. Without it, no one can get inside, unless they are winged creatures such as the robin or the angels (to whom the children compare the robin). The key enhances the private nature of that walled plot of land dedicated to treasured plants and flowers. It evokes ownership, design, responsibility and privilege, or grace.

WHAT MAGIC?

Many times the children refer to "the Magic" with a capital M. This word expresses in the novel the mysterious energies of nature displayed in the varied shapes, colours and scents of the numerous plants growing in the garden, and to some extent also the coordinated fluffy and feathery presence of the many animals encountered in that blessed haven. In another novel for children, the *Harry Potter* series (1997–2007), magic explicitly means the technical mastering of spiritual powers for the sake of influencing the world around. In *The Secret Garden*, "the Magic" is not an ambivalent weapon for the fulfilment of personal ambition. Burnett uses the word for an innocent and disinterested purpose. Her "magic" as seen by the children is contemplative, beneficent and gratuitous. If the novelist had not sadly drifted from Anglicanism to Spiritism, one could interpret her "magic" as divine grace thinly veiled. Burnett's pagan leaning goes almost unnoticed in the narrative stream, thankfully, so that the benevolent force animating plants and animals is plausibly invoked to heal human souls as well (e.g. Colin's inconsolable father), and legitimately seen as a synonym of divine grace. Despite Burnett's positive view of "the Magic", in Anglican England the very expression conveys bigotry, suggesting a connection between "the Magic" or *Hocus-Pocus* and the Roman Catholic formula of Eucharistic consecration in the Holy Sacrifice of the Mass.

> Some believe [Hocus-Pocus] originates from a corruption or parody of the Catholic liturgy of the Eucharist, which contains the phrase 'Hoc est enim corpus meum', meaning This is my body. This explanation goes at least as far back as a 1694 speculation by the Anglican prelate John Tillotson: 'In all probability those common juggling words of hocus pocus are nothing else but a corruption of hoc est corpus, by way of ridiculous imitation of the priests of the Church of Rome in their trick of Transubstantiation.' 10

Thus ends our literal presentation of *The Secret Garden* read as a parable of pre-Anglican England. The novel can be interpreted as

10   https://en.wikipedia.org/wiki/Hocus-pocus #cite_note-6

subliminal Catholicism happily recalled and mysteriously recovered, involving typical elements such as the Virgin Mary, sacrifice, liturgy and grace. We will now use our observations as material to illustrate the needs of England as they appear to us.

## Part Two

---

# THE SPIRITUAL
# MEANING OF
# THE GARDEN

### THE GARDEN OF EDEN

**T**HE HOLY BIBLE describes as a garden the territory where God put Adam and Eve once created. Our first parents were expelled therefrom after the original sin. A cherub with a fiery sword forbade their return to that place of primeval harmony and peace. Subsequently, the lost Garden of Eden came to symbolise human nostalgia for a state of blessedness. Domestic gardens in private houses and allotments are kept primarily for the sake of growing vegetables and flowers. But they also provide spiritual rejuvenation through the pleasurable tilling of one's land, albeit small, and the peace and relaxation experienced when eating or resting within the safe perimeter of one's private natural territory. The garden is a sample of natural creation restored by the redeeming labour of man. Within his well-ordered garden, every man is granted a taste of the original tranquillity, as if back in grace-filled pastures and groves before the first sin. Many religions and spiritual traditions use sacred gardens endowed with a mystical design. Christian revelation proves this intuition correct through the parallel between the Garden of Eden and the Garden of Golgotha. Adam and Eve had committed a sacrilege when plucking and eating the forbidden fruit from the tree of the knowledge of Good and Evil. In reparation, the Cross upon which the New Adam chose to die in atonement for the sins of mankind is the Tree of Life whose branches carried the fruit of salvation, that is, Christ himself.[1] On Easter morning, his Resurrection from the tomb located in the same garden transforms the garden of death and of condemnation into a garden of salvation and of

---

1   Venantius Fortunatus' hymn *Crux Fidelis* beautifully explores this parallel: "Faithful cross, true sign of triumph, Be for all the noblest tree; None in foliage, none in blossom, None in fruit thine equal be; Symbol of the world's redemption, For the weight that hung on thee!"

blessedness. Particularly in Christian lands, ordinary gardens do not simply recall the lost Garden of Eden: they also echo the prophetic recovery of divine friendship wrought by Christ the New Adam in the Garden of Golgotha and Easter. The more elaborate and delineated the garden, the more perceptible its spiritual function.

APPLYING THESE OBSERVATIONS
TO *THE SECRET GARDEN*

Despite being written with ink on paper rather than planted in actual soil, *The Secret Garden* is a valuable illustration of this symbolic and spiritual dimension inherent in any garden. It is not irrelevant to notice that the novelist situated the original catastrophe in the garden. There, its dedicated mistress Lilias, Colin's mother, was killed by a branch falling from the tree under which she liked to rest. The widowed father lost his senses and exiled himself and all posterity from the garden, burying and forgetting the key. This plot reads easily as a transposition of Eve in the Book of Genesis. In the Garden of Eden, her soul was killed by the tree when, having consumed its forbidden fruit, she lost divine grace. Lilias' husband Archibald stands as Adam expelled from Eden, as he carries with him like a curse the memory of spousal harmony destroyed, and he passes on his lethal despair to his posterity. His surname fittingly describes his existential condition: *"craven"* being defined *"lacking the least bit of courage: contemptibly fainthearted; defeated, vanquished"* (cf. Merriam-Webster dictionary). The conjunction with his Christian name is an oxymoron, since *"Archibald"* means *"bold, brave, distinguished."* Craven's faintheartedness, like Adam's fallenness, is a consequence from some original catastrophe caused by evil. Significantly, the only actual snake mentioned in Burnett's story, in Chapter One, hints at the serpentine shape borrowed by Lucifer to tempt Eve in Genesis. The reptile leaves the stage after death has annihilated Mary's entire household:

> But no one came, and as she lay waiting the house seemed to grow more and more silent. She heard something rustling on the matting and when she looked down she saw a little snake gliding along and watching her with eyes like jewels. She was not frightened, because he was a harmless little thing who would not hurt her and he seemed in a hurry to get out of the room. He slipped under the door as she watched him.
>
> 'How queer and quiet it is,' she said. 'It sounds as if there were no one in the bungalow but me and the snake.'

A TALE OF POST-CATHOLIC ENGLAND

If now focussing on national rather than biblical history, this children's book can be read by adults or explained by them to children as a fitting metaphor of England's once cherished Catholic identity. (Sadly this applies to other formerly Christian countries as well.) The land feels deserted, joy is outlawed, and family bonds are severed, since her Dowry has been taken away from Our Lady. Neither the technical efficacy of England's Industrial Revolution nor her political growth as the chief global power of her time through the Empire could make up for the loss of the true faith and Albion's cutting off her daughterly bond from Mother Church. In *The Secret Garden*, healing and peace are granted only once the family members find their way back into the garden. As we have seen, various components of Burnett's story support a Catholic and even a recusant interpretation. The initial motherlessness, the Mary-like quasi mother Susan, the elusive "missel" finally turned real bird as a Christ-friendly robin, the unearthed key and the "Magic" of natural growth and spiritual healing hint at England's longing for a life-giving reappropriation of Mary's motherly queenship, of the Holy Sacrifice of the Mass and of the sacramental economy of grace offered by the Saviour through Church

31

hierarchy. If the young heroine Mary stands for the average soul in post-Catholic Victorian England, no doubt her future looks brighter and more secure after her settling into such a garden. May we reiterate that this interpretation is ours, not the novelist's? We deliberately used her story as a convenient lens to look back at the spiritual needs of England.

## HOW COVID-19 SUSPENDED SACRAMENTAL LIFE

May the reader permit us to broaden the analogy. Catholicism was restored throughout England one year after Burnett's birth in Manchester. The true religion grew and prospered during one century, namely, from 1850 to 1950 or thereabouts. Its doctrine was clear, its liturgy was reverent, its schools taught the faith which the children retained and passed on. Its churches, cathedrals and hospitals were being rebuilt; its abbeys, convents and monasteries were being populated by thousands of novices while flocks of converts, famous or not, were pressing to the doors for reception into the Church or holy baptism. In bitter contrast, since the 1960s, English Catholicism has undergone an accelerated decline. This time, it was not caused by external persecution but by internal factors.

Lately, the Covid-19 crisis felt like watching the past fifty years in fast motion. Since the 1970s, the number of priests per laity had dropped constantly and churches were shut down at an ominous pace. But starting in March 2020, with unanimity reminiscent of Penal Times, *all* Catholic churches were closed overnight for months, many not reopening. The young and the converts could not be baptised; the dying were not assisted by priests; the dead were buried without family or nearly; those engaged could not wed; and devout Catholics were kept out from their familiar churches, chapels and shrines. The public offering of the Holy Sacrifice of the Mass was forbidden altogether. If, to name but a few of our glorious martyrs, St Thomas More, St John Fisher and St Margaret Clitheroe (a laywoman pressed to death for having harboured priests offering Holy Mass in her attic) had visited England during the Covid-19 crisis, would they not have questioned this lockdown of sacramental grace?[2] Catholics and converts deprived of access to sacred places and sacred actions felt like young Mary in *The Secret Garden* on arriving at Misselthwaite

2   *Religious Freedom in the Time of the Pandemic* by Piotr Mazurkiewicz, Institute of Political Science and Public Administration, Cardinal Stefan Wyszynski University in Warsaw, 3 February 2021. Accessed on 8th July 2021 via https://www.mdpi.com/2077-1444/12/2/103/htm.

Manor. Everything was bleakly shut up. No one in the estate seemed to know of a garden, that is, a place of solace and spiritual sustenance. Similarly, during the Covid-19 crisis, all churches were locked. In none of them was access to the sacraments permitted.

By chance, or rather, by providence, some of the faithful heard of places where the sacraments could be received with due precautions. They travelled longer distances to gain access to the life of grace through Confession, Holy Communion, or silent adoration of the Eucharistic Saviour. In certain churches, though, the administering of Holy Communion was loaded with so many sanitary rules as to lack the minimum reverence necessary for a fruitful reception and peaceful thanksgiving.[3]

---

3 Letter *Let us return to the Eucharist with joy!*, dated 15th August 2020, to the Presidents of the Episcopal Conferences of the Catholic Church on the celebration of the liturgy during and after the Covid-19 pandemic, by Robert Cardinal Sarah, Prefect of the Congregation for Divine Worship and the Discipline of the Sacraments: "due attention to hygiene and safety regulations cannot lead to the sterilisation of gestures and rites, to the instilling, even unconsciously, of fear and insecurity in the faithful… It is up to the prudent but firm action of the Bishops to ensure that the participation of the faithful in the celebration of the Eucharist is not reduced by public authorities to a 'gathering', and is not considered comparable or even subordinate to forms of recreational activities… Liturgical norms are not matters on which civil authorities can legislate, but only the competent ecclesiastical authorities (cf. *Sacrosanctum Concilium*, 22).

Heartbroken, many regular communicants were led to abstain rather than partake in services where sanitary protocols had replaced the hallowed rubrics of the liturgy. Browsing the Internet or enquiring with their friends over the phone, some Catholics heard for the first time of the traditional Latin Mass. They cautiously watched broadcast services and homilies. They felt like "Mistress Mary" peeping through the keyhole into the "Secret Garden." For many Catholics confined at home, the screens of family desktops and of smartphones glowed like as many vistas into the exotic world of the holy traditions of the Church.[4] To their surprise, the liturgy looked reverent,

The participation of the faithful in the liturgical celebrations should be facilitated, but without improvised ritual experiments and in full respect of the norms contained in the liturgical books which govern their conduct. In the liturgy, an experience of sacredness, holiness and beauty that transfigures, gives a foretaste of the harmony of the eternal blessedness. Care should therefore be taken to ensure the dignity of the places, the sacred furnishings, the manner of celebration, according to the authoritative instruction of the Second Vatican Council... The faithful should be recognised as having the right to receive the Body of Christ and to worship the Lord present in the Eucharist in the manner provided for, without limitations that go even beyond what is provided for by the norms of hygiene issued by public authorities or Bishops ... " Original text on http://www.cultodivino.va/content/cultodivino/it/documenti/lettere-circolari/torniamo-con-gioia-all-eucaristia--15-agosto-2020-.html
4   The traditional liturgical channel LiveMass.net had half a million visitors during Lent and Easter 2020.

not artificial; and the doctrine sounded clear and nourishing, rather than harsh and abstruse. When the Covid-19 restrictions eased up, these Catholics ventured for the first time to traditional services, having duly checked that such Mass centres were in good standing with their dioceses. Despite the absence of congregational singing and the impossibility of meeting with parishioners after Holy Mass as per the Covid-19 regulations, the newcomers felt their initial unease turn into spiritual comfort, and their perplexity into soothing recollection. After a while, they wondered how a liturgical setting so new to them could evince such blessed homeliness.

## Part Three

# WHAT HAPPENED AT ST MARY'S CHURCH

### THANK YOU, DEAR ARCHBISHOP!

FIVE YEARS BEFORE Covid-19, in Advent 2015, some ordinary Catholics undertook an unexpected journey. It took place within a neo-Gothic church built 130 years earlier by several Pugin architects. In that beautiful church, Mass in English was taking place daily, offered by a resident parish priest according to the customs of the time. For about forty years, a rectangular wooden table[1] and a slim lectern had been standing on a

---

1  Not sealed to the floor, never anointed, it bore no consecration crosses, displayed no Christian patterns and harboured no sacred relics.

wide carpeted platform set up in the middle of the church nave, all across the central aisle, from column to column. Upon it, facing the congregation, the ministerial priest presided over the Eucharistic liturgy; the lay readers proclaimed the lessons and intercessory prayers before assisting the celebrant in distributing consecrated Bread and Wine to the people standing in line.

In 2015, for want of priests, the provident Archbishop of that diocese invited a traditional fraternity to take over that church rather than have it turned into flats or shops. Neighbouring churches offered ample provision of Masses in English for those who preferred. Most of the congregation remained at St Mary's however, now established by the Archbishop as a "shrine church" (instead of "parish church") for anyone to visit and attend if they so wished. People became used to Holy Mass in Latin, looking with the priest celebrant towards the altar of sacrifice like the Hebrew people followed Moses towards the Promised Land. Translations were provided, and explanations were offered regularly about the rich symbols of the traditional Roman liturgy. Three months later, understanding by the laity was further facilitated when the wide carpeted platform and the rectangular table were removed from the nave while, simultaneously, a high altar was restored at the far back, under the tabernacle. A whole generation had only known the main aisle of the building leading as far as the platform in the nave, where it abruptly ended. They had always assumed that the table on the carpet was the focus. Never had they looked at the wide platform as a later accretion; even less had the thought ever occurred to them of questioning its shape, its style, its presence or its purpose. Worship is naturally conservative and worshippers rightly expect to be guided and led, not to pass judgements or to suggest improvements. In consequence, the vast platform had always fitted in the general perception of the people as simply part of the way their church was laid out.

VISION RESTORED

The disappearance of the platform caused a double shock. The first realisation was that the church interior had taken an entirely new outlook, as if loaded with a different meaning. The second realisation was that this difference felt promising. The central aisle had sprung by one quarter further down, now reaching the marble altar rail previously concealed. The altar rail had gates, one discovered, which opened into the former backstage of the platform, now effortlessly drawing attention to itself. Fittingly, one observed, not only the central aisle but the entire perspective of the building now converged on that hitherto remote area — the sanctuary — suddenly endowed with unsuspected visibility and prominence. Across it, in three flights, seven steps guided the gaze of the worshipper toward a wide rectangular shape draped in precious material: the high altar restored as the sacrificial pedestal to the tabernacle, central point of the entire edifice. Right above it, a high canopy rose upon thin marble columns, all the way up to the vast rose window through which sunlight poured in. For the first time, the visitor experienced a seamless sweep of his gaze all along the central aisle, through the altar rail, across the sanctuary, up to the altar and further up along the high canopy to the majestic stained glass window whence colourful light flooded. The silent journey of one's pilgrim eyes from floor to window carried one's soul from earth to heaven in one swing, via the place of sacrifice. With a hint of embarrassment, one then realised that the wide carpeted platform, now vanished, had never belonged to the original design of the edifice. Rather, it had stood in the way. For forty years it had diverted the complex architectural communication. It had obscured the mystical perspective. It had concealed the garden, as we will now explain.

## ST MARY'S SANCTUARY IS A GARDEN

What garden? As they walked down the central aisle at St Mary's Shrine Church, attentive worshippers might have been struck by an optical illusion. Above the tabernacle, the top of the stone pinnacle seemed to move, as if actually rising against the circular Lady window set above the reredos. As a rose within the wider rose, that stain-glass centre depicted the face of Our Lady crowned as Queen, surrounded with red rose petals. The closer one stood to the carpeted platform, the nearer the pinnacle grew below the centre of the Lady window. But as long as the platform had stood in the way, no one had suspected that pinnacle and Lady window might ever meet. This changed once the aisle had been cleared from the wide platform. On proceeding further down one could see the pinnacle soar higher and higher above the tabernacle until, before the wondering eyes of the observer now standing right outside the altar rail, the stem of carved stone reached the central disc of lit glass. Mindful of one's position right before God in the tabernacle, one would fall on one's knees in adoration of the divine presence. This lowering of one's stature rewarded the worshipper with a grace-filled discovery as the stone stem finally came to rest in the very centre of the rose window depicting the face of the Blessed Virgin Mary. One delighted in the red petals surrounding her lovely features in reference to her title in the litany: "Mystical rose." Then, and only then, was the luminous "rose" visually connected with her mineral "stem." Now it lived. Flowers don't last once cut. But those kept on their stems unceasingly translate in colours and fragrances the unseen vigour of the sap drawn from the soil through the roots. The Lady window depicted this flowering through a network of branches, connecting to the central figure of Our Lady her female prefigurations in the Old Testament: Eve, Rebecca, Rachel, Bathsheba, Judith and Esther. The entire Lady window shone as a family tree, or a family rosebush, rather, whose choicest bud was divine, Christ the Lord, Son of the Virgin.

Still on his knees by the altar rail, the worshipper now noticed how the vegetal theme spread throughout the sanctuary. Right in front of him, the tabernacle was surrounded by ten large marble passion flowers, with marble wheat and grapes supporting the thin Eucharistic tabor above. The central canopy was designed like a vigorous sheaf reaching for the light. On either side, the thin columns of two lower canopies also displayed budding tops, like midsummer shoots springing out of neatly trimmed topiary shapes. Half silver, half beeswax, the thin and high "big six" candles on their candlesticks figured an intermediary stage in the mysterious conversion of inanimate matter into living stems. Under the side canopies, elaborate groups of the Nativity and of the Adoration of the Magi were supported by shelves adorned with sculpted leaves, branches and berries. Petals and buds covered the structural elements of the high and wide reredos. The gradines at its bottom were stamped with flowery "M" letters after the initial of Our Lady's name. At the far ends, standing in ornate niches, St Joseph held a lily and Our Lady was crowned with fleur-de-lis. From the stained glass and stonework, vegetation spread across the floor, whose exquisite tiles displayed Marian lilies, their white petals spreading above their green stems and leaves and their brown roots against a blue background. Vegetation also climbed on the wooden choir stalls, whose ends carried carved pomegranates bursting with seeds. Even the candles signalling the small consecration crosses on the walls all around were set in iron holders wrought as sinuous branches. The gates into the liturgical "garden" (or sanctuary) introduced the vegetal theme with an intricate pattern of branches in wrought iron, while all along the "garden fence," that is, the Communion rail, round-ended quadrifoliums (four-petalled patterns) alternated with pointed ones, in between marble pillars whose tops displayed sculpted leaves. Truly, this place was a holy garden, Mary's own garden. Winged creatures dwelt in it, with angels of various sizes posted in every corner, balustrade and niche — and even birds: a wooden eagle as lectern, and stone carved raven and dove as emblems of the saintly siblings Benedict and Scholastica.

## THEOLOGICAL FITTINGNESS OF THE LITURGICAL GARDEN

To what purpose, one might then wonder, had the inspired architect skilfully impressed such a multifaceted depiction of life throughout this part of the building? The answer is given when the Sacristy bell heralds the Entrance procession. Preceded by his clerical retinue walking in hierarchal order, the priest walks down the central aisle. The ornate Sanctuary gates open slowly enough for the worshipper to read on the left one the Latin words: *"Introibo ad"* and on the right *"Altare Dei"* — *"I will go in to the altar of God."* Those are the first words uttered by the celebrant at every traditional Latin Mass after blessing himself. Access into the sanctuary, the Holy of Holies where the God-Man truly dwells, is granted for one purpose only, namely, the unbloody re-enactment of the unique Sacrifice of the Cross on the liturgical altar by the priest acting in the very person of Christ. No one treads into this sacred precinct unless his mission pertains to the dutiful performing of the Eucharistic Sacrifice or its preparation. The Holy Sacrifice of the Mass is par excellence the mystery of divine life restored by Christ's Passion and Death, and communicated to all believers as to branches grafted into the Vine divine, or as members united with their Head. The Most Precious Blood of the Lamb of God, Jesus the Saviour of all men, is the sap of everlasting life flowing from the altar through the priestly ministry, down to the faithful kneeling along the altar rail for Holy Communion.

How utterly fitting, one then realises, the design of the sanctuary as God's sacrificial garden. There, and only there, is the Garden of Eden restored, and even improved. No more desolated through human sin, the Garden is cleansed through the red dew flowing from the pierced side of the New Adam Our Lord, offered on the Tree of the Cross as the Victim of reconciliation of all men with the divine Father. The Garden of Eden had become for us the Garden of spiritual Death (soon causing physical death), until the saving Sacrifice of Jesus Christ turned it into fertile land again on Easter morning. This was made possible through God's merciful design of assuming our human nature in the Incarnation of his Son. When the Immaculate Virgin uttered her *Fiat* in humble response to the archangel's tidings, she procured the grafting of our human nature into the divinity.

The Mass is ended. The worshipper now stands up and walks away from the altar rail where he had been contemplating the inspired design of the architecture so skilfully echoing God's plan of redemption. This sacred mystery of God's benevolence for our sinful race eliciting our filial cooperation is eloquently depicted, the worshipper recalls, in the architectural device of the mineral stem — the pinnacle of the canopy sheltering the tabernacle — reaching Our Lady's comely face in the circular stained glass window as one devoutly kneels down in adoration. Yes, this precious Sanctuary is God's Garden and Our Lady's, where Adam's progeny learn to stand (on their knees) among the lilies, until they fly with angels in the afterlife.

## EUCHARISTIC ADORATION

This truth shows splendidly on Sunday afternoons at St Mary's Shrine. Then, starting with Sung Vespers, sunlight irradiates the great Lady rose window. From their choir stalls, clerics melodiously alternate the sacred psalms across the sanctuary. During the *Magnificat*, the three ministers wearing colourful copes incense the altar. Mingling with the perfume of actual lilies arranged in silvery vases upon the gradines, the aromatic smoke of incense slowly rises up the colossal stem of the stone canopy above the tabernacle and reaches the wide stain-glass "flower," the Lady window, as if men's offering of holy fragrance reciprocated God's gift of sunlight flooding from above down to the flowery tiles of the sacred precinct.

Eucharistic Benediction follows. On their knees in the pews, the faithful adore the sacred Host displayed through the gilded porthole of the monstrance set upon the white-clothed altar. Behind and above it, does not the high and wide sanctuary wall echo the shape of the monstrance? Indeed the Eucharistic vessel combines three parts, namely, a circular pane of glass surrounded with metal rays, mounted on a thin vertical rod, itself set on a wide base. Symmetrically, set on the wide altar as its base, the stem-like canopy rises as a stone rod, supporting at its top the round Lady window. On a late summer afternoon in particular, the sun shows as a disc of fire enshrined within the round stained glass, evoking a large-scale equivalent of the sacred Host displayed in the circular lunette, held behind the glass of the monstrance below. What a striking analogy of shapes! Was it designed on purpose, one might ask? Did the architect Pugin, a Catholic convert, or the priests commissioning him, intend this correspondence between architecture and liturgy? Even though fortuitous for men, for God such a design is not accidental. The divine Creator once sent a bright star all the way to the cave of Bethlehem, where His eternal Son was being born of a Woman. Nothing more consistent then, than to bring another star within the framed stained glass in whose centre shines the same Woman, the true Mother of God. That other star stops above the altar where the small monstrance stands, in whose centre the Sun of Justice radiates Eucharistic graces.

Lest some of our readers deem such liturgical fervour somehow remote from the concerns and passions of this world, let us offer the following excursion by way of illustrative contrast. It will show that unity, sought by all men, is truly granted them in St Mary's sanctuary and in other such sacred precincts. A secular event, then, occurred nearly at the same time as the sacred one just described. Within hours, during the Euro 2020 final on Sunday 11th July 2021, the whole of Great-Britain[2]

---

2    The Euro 2020 final England vs. Italy [N. B. delayed until 11th July 2021 due to Covid-19] was the most-watched event in UK history with 42 million viewers (television and Internet combined).

watched another sphere, one made of leather rather than fire, framed into the goal of Wembley Stadium. At the last penalty, eighty-four million British eyes (for sixty-seven million inhabitants) followed the final flight of the ball from an Italian striker's foot into the national goal — where for a second it stood still, and the world with it... Where does such unanimity ever occur? When are the eyes and hearts of an entire nation ever riveted on a mere speck of matter as if the people's salvation depended on it? From a natural perspective, social unity was manifested at that moment, most strikingly. And yet, as any Catholic knows, much more is offered to men. Souls are called to undefeated and everlasting union when focussing on the Eucharistic Sun, the same Jesus whose face they will behold, when at the end of history he comes with might and glory.[3] On that sunny evening of the Euro final, if ever flying over London,

---

3  "For as lightning cometh out of the east, and appeareth even into the west: so shall the coming of the Son of man be. Wheresoever the body shall be, there shall the eagles also be gathered together... And then shall appear the sign of the Son of man in heaven: and then shall all tribes of the earth mourn: and they shall see the Son of man coming in the clouds of heaven with much power and majesty. And he shall send his angels with a trumpet, and a great voice: and they shall gather together his elect from the four winds, from the farthest parts of the heavens to the utmost bounds of them" (Mt 24:27–28; 30–31).

49

would some holy angels have mistaken the Wembley temple of football for a gigantic monstrance: its oval silvery frame enshrining a rectangular emerald against a ruby background? Since the angels are Catholic, they would readily share in the joy and fraternity occasioned by sport events (especially after seventeen months of social isolation). But they would also stress that unity among men is truly found only in God — God known, loved and served — a truth nowhere better experienced and practiced by us humans than during Eucharistic worship.

When at St Mary's altar the priest blesses them with the shining vessel, all believe that through it divine graces flow into their souls more generously even than the sunbeams illumine their eyes through the stained glass above. At that instant, shared Eucharistic faith connects all most intimately: adults and children, clergy and laity, men and women know themselves to be made one another's limbs within the mystical Body of Christ, His Holy Church, whose Eucharistic Heart is beating before them. The metal beams of silver and gold springing out of the central body of the monstrance imitate natural sunbeams emitted by our star. At least, so does it appear to the eyes of flesh. To one's soul's eyes, reaching beyond photons, in this circulation of light the sunbeams are but the imitation, while the streams of grace invisible are the original. Indeed, the summer sun whose light bathes the church interior during Benediction is but a sign, a symbol merely meant by God to delight little children (looking a bit tired over there in the third pew) with a foretaste of His ardent charity. Across the Lady window, the floral network of convoluted stems figuring Our Lady's ancestors in the Old Testament is a mere artistic projection, worshippers realise, of their own spiritual kinship across the pews and sanctuary. They give thanks to God for such an association whereby, pagans and unbelievers as they or their fathers once were, they are now grafted into the true Vine or olive tree of Jesus Christ in His Church, as Scripture teaches: "*thou wert cut out of the wild olive tree, which is natural to thee; and, contrary to nature, were grafted into the good olive tree*" (Rom 11:24). Worshippers beg God to allow them to bear fruit of faith, hope and charity. Aptly combined within St Mary's garden, sacred architecture and liturgical forms display this invisible grafting of souls accomplished by the divine "gardener."

This truth is confirmed on Good Friday, the only day when the main altar is stripped from its three cloths and ornate frontal. Then, against the backdrop below the tabletop or *mensa* of the altar, a carved vase becomes visible, whence more branches spring. This pattern duplicates in marble the stained glass depiction described earlier, high above it on the great rose window. It stresses an essential truth: that we are members of one another because we are grafted in Christ and such grafting begun through the Incarnation of the Word Eternal in Our Lady's womb (cf. the Marian branches stemming out of the glass vase on the rose window); later to be completed when the New Adam redeemed us through his death on the Cross (cf. the marble branches springing from the urn under the altar). How fitting that the latter depiction should be visible only on Good Friday, when the solemn commemoration of the Passion and Death of the Lord excludes even the celebration of Holy Mass. Worshippers then realise that Holy Mass makes them members of one another[4] only because Christ died for us all on Golgotha.[5]

---

4   "So we being many, are one body in Christ, and every one members one of another" — Rom 12:5.
5   "The chalice of benediction, which we bless, is it not the communion of the blood of Christ? And the bread, which we break, is it not the partaking of the body of the Lord? For we, being many, are one bread, one body, all that partake of one bread" — 1 Cor 16–17.

*Part Four*

---

# TILLING THE GARDEN
# OF HOLY TRADITIONS

ET US NOW EX-
amine the tools and
techniques applied to till St
Mary's garden.

### THE "MISSAL THRUSHES" HAVE LANDED

A few months after the traditional Latin
Mass had started again at St Mary's Church, a
cloud of squarish birds became visible across
the pews. Mostly black, some beige and white,
they were not called "missel thrushes" like in
*The Secret Garden* but "hand missals." That spe-
cies, once very common, had become extinct
for decades according to experts. A quiet gag-
gle of about two hundred of them had now
happily settled at St Mary's, meritoriously

tamed by the congregation to whom they had become valued companions. We are referring of course to the traditional hand books to follow Holy Mass, "like in the old days." Latin and English were displayed side by side on every page, with useful explanations about the ceremonies taking place, about the lives of the saints and many prayers, devotions and rituals designed to accompany every Christian all along his earthly journey. Like peacocks fan out their spectacular tail feathers, the "missal thrushes" obligingly displayed the many treasures printed on thin paper across their 2,248 pages, including:

- ⚜ All the Masses of the Liturgical Year, in Latin with English translation (Biblical texts are from the Douay-Rheims), according to the Roman Calendar of 1962 — Temporal and Sanctoral Cycles and accompanying rites (Blessing of Ashes, Blessing of Palms, Chrism Mass, and the Blessing of Holy Oils, etc)
- ⚜ Ordinary of the Mass, in Latin with English translation
- ⚜ Liturgical Calendar
- ⚜ Table of Moveable Feasts up to AD 2066
- ⚜ Complete Holy Week Liturgy of 1962 (including the Office of Tenebrae)
- ⚜ Common Masses of the Saints and the Blessed Virgin
- ⚜ Feasts celebrated in particular places and in certain religious congregations

⚜ Votive Masses for the days of the week
⚜ Sixteen Votive Masses for various occasions
⚜ Masses for the Dead (including infants), Complete Burial Service, Prayers for the Dead
⚜ Marriage Service and Nuptial Mass
⚜ The Churching of Women
⚜ Kyriale, in traditional Gregorian chant notation, including:
　　Tones for the most common Ordinaries: I (*Lux et Origo*), IV (*Cunctipotens Genitor Deus*), VIII (*De Angelis*), IX (*Cum Jubilo*), XI (*Orbis Factor*), XXVII (Sundays of Advent & Lent), XVIII (*Deus Genitor Alme*)
⚜ Tones for the *Asperges* and the *Vidi Aquam*
⚜ Tones for the *Credo*: I, II, III and IV
⚜ Vespers for Sundays and Feasts
⚜ Compline for Sundays
⚜ Hymns and chants for Exposition and Benediction of the Blessed Sacrament
⚜ Anthems to the Blessed Virgin Mary
⚜ Litany of the Saints
⚜ Various Devotions and Prayers including favourite Litanies, the Way of the Cross, prayers of the Rosary and others
⚜ Morning and Evening Prayers
⚜ Devotions for Confession
⚜ Devotions for Holy Communion
⚜ *Te Deum Laudamus*
⚜ The Itinerary or Office before a Journey
⚜ Various Blessings
⚜ An explanation of "The Liturgy or Public Worship of the Catholic and Roman Church"
⚜ An Abridgement of Christian Doctrine.

No wonder that the laity agreed to pay a high price (even though bulk orders attracted substantial discounts) for the newly printed leather-bound volumes: such an investment in one's supernatural life was worth every penny.[1] Cheap and well-designed booklets were also available for beginners, displaying small sketches of the various stages of Holy Mass to guide the worshippers.

SEASONS AND FRAGRANCES IN THE GARDEN

As months went by, newcomers became more familiar with the traditional liturgy displayed in so fitting architecture. They felt like migrants settling in a land once foreign. They learnt to recognise the seasons as displayed by the liturgical colours of the priestly vestments, of the altar frontal and of the chalice veils. Purple was the colour of autumn. It spread throughout the sanctuary for penitential times: for Advent and from Septuagesima until the

---

1 No edition of a hand missal is perfect. We eventually chose the Baronius one because it provides the English but also the Latin texts for the ordinary of the Mass and also for the Propers (texts and prayers specific to each saint or feast). The publisher's choice to include the Propers for all English-speaking dioceses on various continents makes the volume a bit thick. Its useful introductions to every feast and Sunday are more succinct than in the St Andrew's edition for instance. The list of contents given above is borrowed from the Baronius missal. Cf. https://www.baroniuspress.com/.

Sacred Triduum, but also four times a year for the Ember days, for the vigil of saints and of main feasts, and for penitential votive Masses for the sick, for a happy death, against pestilence etc. The secret garden of sacred traditions was shrouded in black for funeral Masses and votive Masses for the Holy Souls in Purgatory. It looked like winter, when death apparent shelters life deep within. It turned into vernal green for the time after Pentecost all the way until Advent. Scarlet indicated summer, as the crimson shade of holy charity caught like flame on Pentecost, at Palm Sunday and on the many feasts of martyrs. Rose gleamed as briefly and tenderly as the flower by the same name, on *Gaudete* and *Laetare* Sundays. Finally, white expressed the triumphant flowing of divine grace in most feasts of the Lord Jesus, of Our Lady and of non-martyred clerics, religious, doctors and saintly women. Recent worshippers watched with awe and peaceful jubilation the solemn choreography of the priests or even bishops, of deacons, subdeacons, acolytes, lectors, thurifers and masters of ceremony across the holy of holies at every holy Mass, at priestly Ordinations and Confirmations, at Eucharistic Benediction and even, thrice a day at Lauds, Vespers and Compline, when psalms of praise and intercession are sung to the Holy Trinity, culminating in the three canticles heralding

God's Incarnation: St Zachary's *Benedictus*, Our Lady's *Magnificat* and St Simeon's *Nunc Dimittis*.

## THE SACRAMENTALS

The faithful came forward to harvest special graces through the various sacramentals of the Church according to the liturgical season: novenas to the Immaculate Conception in December, or to the Holy Ghost before Pentecost; *Rorate* Masses in Advent, offered before dawn with hundreds of candles lit instead of electric light; public consecrations to the Sacred Heart and to the Immaculate Heart of Mary; weekly Stations of the Cross; daily Holy Rosary; Epiphany Water (a two-hour long rite of blessing) and blessing of chalk to sign the lintels of their houses; provision of exorcised holy water mingled with exorcised salt; medals of St Benedict and Miraculous medals; Brown scapulars on the feast of Our Lady of Mount Carmel (16th July); blessing of throats on St Blaise's feast; aspersion with ashes made out of the burnt palms from the previous Holy Week; Palm Sunday procession, Tenebrae sung around the sanctuary hearse every morning during the Sacred Triduum; stripping of all four altars on Maundy Thursday and adoration late in the night at the Altar of Repose, candlelit and covered with flowers; Solemn Good Friday liturgy; outdoor New Fire and long Easter vigil; May processions and crowning of Our Lady's statue; daily visits to the nearby cemetery to obtain the liberation of holy souls from Purgatory over the eight days from All Saints onward; and last but not least, penitential processions against pestilence, as well as joyful ones such as the Candlemas procession and the Corpus Christi procession, in or outside the church as circumstances permitted.

## MULTIPLE INTERACTIONS ACROSS THE LITURGICAL GARDEN

Even without changing places in the church, to their surprise worshippers discovered an unsuspected depth of participation in the sacred mysteries despite and across the distance between their pews and the sanctuary. The complexity of liturgical symbols, the mystery of the sacred Latin language, the constant focus of ministers and congregation on the tabernacle and the altar enlightened their intellects, enriched their imagination, refined their mystical experience and fed their souls with supernatural abundance, taste and peace. They felt as if their supernatural senses were being gently awakened by the homely splendour of the traditional liturgy. They started detecting some hitherto unsuspected network of invisible interactions. It consisted not only of the responses of the clergy from the choir

stalls on the Gospel side to the ones opposite;
or those of the congregation in the nave to
the celebrant at the altar. With and through
those, communication reached further, as the
fragrance of incense rose up the floral canopy
toward the Lady window, a vertical dialogue
of supplication and mercy between earth and
heaven became perceptible. Holy angels, holy
souls and saints invited the living on earth into
a moving and jubilant polyphony of faith, as
we will now explain.

The nine choirs of angels were not only
carved statues around the Sanctuary. No, they
were actively involved in the sacred liturgy,
as demonstrated in the double Confiteor, the
Gloria, the Sanctus, the Incensation Prayer and,
last but not least, the votive Mass of the Holy
Angels and the separate feasts of Archangels
St Michael, St Raphael and St Gabriel. The
holy angels were at work, assisting, guiding
and protecting the mortals as they had served
the Son of Man at his Nativity, in the desert,
at Gethsemane and forever in heaven. The traditional liturgy showed that the existence of
the holy angels was real and their involvement
constant. Equally, the holy souls in Purgatory
were prayed for at every Mass with earnest
conviction that the power of Christ's Sacrifice
and the intercession of the living alleviate the
sufferings of those undergoing purification

after death. In brotherly reciprocity, the living hoped for the prayers of the holy souls to God on their behalf, at least on entering heaven once cleansed from venial sins. Such solidarity between earth and Purgatory was relied upon and implemented as a constant feature of the traditional Mass. Lastly, the saints in heaven were prayed unceasingly. St John the Baptist, Sts Peter and Paul, St Joseph and the many early martyrs were invoked by name at every Holy Mass. In addition, the richness of the liturgical cycle endowed nearly each day with several saints whose virtues inspired and whose intercession helped the living. Newcomers experienced the vertical dimension of holy Church: the necessary care for those in need still on earth was complemented and elevated by the manifold interaction with the holy angels, the holy souls and the saints.

Those come recently to the traditional holy Mass had heard of such features before, of course, unless they were converts. But here they found them combined, orchestrated and bearing fruit in their lives as never before. The training of their supernatural senses now allowed worshippers to take a deeper part in that mysterious communication within the one holy Church of God — Church Militant on earth, Church Suffering in Purgatory and Church Triumphant in Heaven.

PRIESTS AND FAMILIES

In the name of Christ and of holy Church, priests would teach the faith of ages with clarity, authority and persuasion. They would dress and be seen to behave at all times in accordance with the doctrine they had received and transmitted. They would explain the mysterious yet objective workings of divine grace amidst sinful worldliness. Words such as indulgences, reparation, atonement, intercession, sacrifice, merits, graces and thanksgiving were gradually understood as expressing crucial and beautiful realities, now revealed through faith and made use of in supernatural confidence. This prompted a hundred penitents every week to kneel in the confessional for an intimate encounter with the God of mercy, speaking to them through the voice of their priest behind the screen. The number of daily communicants increased by one third, and the Sunday congregation by two thirds.

Among them were a growing number of families, sometimes large ones. Children felt that the liturgy spoke to their senses and touched their hearts. How could the little ones not have felt warmly welcomed, when in the sanctuary the carved reredos displayed on either side of the tabernacle the wonder of an Infant God, first in Christ's Nativity, and then in the Adoration of the Magi? Parents also appreciated the constant encouragements of family life received from the pulpit, in the confessional and through the various adult groups. The glory of holy Matrimony was visually manifest in the impressive statues of St Joseph and Our Lady, standing in ornate niches on either side of the tabernacle where their divine Son dwelt Eucharistically. Homilies and spiritual direction explained the rights and duties of Christian parents and children, while frequent pro-life initiatives weaved the protection of the most vulnerable into the very fabric of daily devotion at St Mary's, whether with prayers before a large-size replica of the image of Our Lady of Guadalupe, or through prayerful witness in the streets. Grown and young men were proud to serve in the various liturgies while women helped with sacred linens, flowers, cleaning, stewarding or singing. Young adults of either sex were guided to discern the holy will of God for them: if not to consecrated life, then to family life. Individuals and families joined in significant numbers a confraternity[2] dedicated to praying for priestly vocations and ministry. Young men were admitted into seminaries, young women into convents, while young couples would get

---

2   The Confraternity of St Peter is a 7,400-strong international prayer network for priestly vocations: https://fssp.org.uk/about-the-confraternity/.

married to raise children to people heaven with new saints.

MUSIC

This latter aspect of the sacred liturgy at St Mary's struck newcomers. They knew about Gregorian chant, perhaps having heard some when visiting a monastery, and possibly recalled that it was to *"be given pride of place in liturgical services,"* as stated at Vatican II.[3] But never had they encountered Gregorian chant as the normal musical setting at parish sung Masses. Its peaceful and soothing melodies connected the worshippers with the early Christians in the ages of faith. In addition, polyphonic compositions by Palestrina or Byrd were readily performed by the Shrine choir. One might well have listened to such pieces on the radio or even at some concerts, but the impact was enormously deeper when experienced as part of the sacred liturgy for which these masterpieces had been composed in the first place. In every garden, secret or not, the songs of mistle thrushes, robins and nightingales gave glory to God unbeknownst to the birds. But in the liturgical garden of holy traditions at St Mary's, humans praised God knowingly, with words inspired by him, modulated according to sacred melodies that

---

3  Cf. *Sacrosanctum Concilium* # 116.

gloriously reverberated among carved angels and alabaster flowers, as refined echoes of the invisible truths revealed by God and celebrated in the sacred mysteries.

Worshippers at St Mary's Shrine came to appreciate the floral pattern of sculptures, stained glass, carved wood and floor tiles decorating the Sanctuary. The germination, the budding, the flowing, the flying and singing, the lively fruitfulness depicted by the church architect most adequately displayed before one's bodily eyes the invisible circulation of love and grace between earth and heaven from bottom to top of the sanctuary. The sacred space was revealed as a stairway to heaven, as a catalyst for contrition and mercy, as a field daily harvested, as an orchard rich in fruit, through which the tears of penitents were collected by angels and the most precious Blood of the Lamb was spread upon wounded souls gradually healed, purified, strengthened, enlightened and rejuvenated by such salutary balm. Such was the secret garden of holy traditions into which, from the nave and Communion rail, pilgrims to St Mary's Shrine reverently gazed, spiritually plunged and sacramentally fed.

## Part Five

---

# RETURN TO PARADISE

### RECAPITULATION

N THE BEGIN-
ning of this little essay,
we have used the 1911 children's novel *The Secret Garden*
as a lens to evoke what England
lost through the Protestant revolution and the
establishment of Anglicanism. We observed
that the Covid-19 crisis accelerated the Catholic decline numerically evidenced from the
1960s. The 2020–2021 pandemic almost totally
suspended sacramental life throughout the
country and closed all churches overnight. Hin-
drances to a reverent reception of the sacraments in most parishes prompted some believers to experience the traditional liturgy,
wherever allowed by the bishops. These

newcomers discovered an unsuspected wealth of liturgical symbols and spiritual realities which proved a providential help to their souls. Coming across such treasures felt to them as if walking into some secret garden. They marvelled at how eloquently the church architecture, the music and the doctrine expressed the Good News of salvation. Grateful for the Christian knowledge acquired previously, they were gladdened to see it displayed in the traditional setting with ravishing harmony, unsuspected beauty and joyful efficacy. Like Mistress Mary, the young heroine in Burnett's novel, they felt privileged to have been admitted into such a *Secret Garden*, a mysterious shrine whose carved flowers and sculpted birds echoed the luxuriance of divine grace flowing into souls through the gestures, colours and music of liturgical actions performed with reverence and explained adequately. The holy traditions of the Church appeared to many as a blessed garden, a haven of decorous piety.

PARADISE REGAINED?

To devout souls condemned to dwell month after month within the narrow confines of their homes according to Covid-19 rules, sacramental deprivation felt like Purgatory, if not like hell, and a glimpse or taste of traditional liturgies looked like Paradise. We mentioned

earlier the rich symbolism of the enclosed garden in diverse cultures throughout history,
based on nostalgia for the idyllic Garden of
Eden. Those newcomers who discovered the
holy traditions of the Church, first within
the frame of their computer screens and later
when kneeling by the Communion rails of the
same churches, have often felt as if they had
stepped into Paradise. Something precious and
vital for their souls, they knew, was enclosed,
preserved, enshrined and displayed within
such holy traditions. As it happens, the words
*paradise* and *tradition* sound very similar in
Greek, although etymologically unrelated.
In the original Greek, our word "paradise"
spells παράδεισος, transliterated as *parádeisos*.
It bears a suggestive resemblance with the
word παράδοση used frequently in the New
Testament in particular, and transliterated as
*parádosi*, meaning "tradition."

The *Free Dictionary* provides this interesting
history of the word *paradise*:[1]

From an etymological perspective at least,
paradise is located in ancient Iran — for it
is there that the word *paradise* ultimately
originates. The old Iranian language Aves-
tan had a noun *pairidaēza-*, "a wall enclosing
a garden or orchard," which is composed

---

1   https://www.thefreedictionary.com/paradises,
accessed 8th July 2021.

of *pairi-*, "around," and *daēza-* "wall." The adverb and preposition *pairi* is related to the equivalent Greek form *peri*, as in *perimeter*. *Daēza-* comes from the Indo-European root *\*dheigh-*, "to mould, form, shape." Zoroastrian religion encouraged maintaining arbours, orchards, and gardens, and even the kings of austere Sparta were edified by seeing the Great King of Persia planting and maintaining his own trees in his own garden. Xenophon, a Greek mercenary soldier who spent some time in the Persian army and later wrote histories, recorded the *pairidaēza-* surrounding the orchard as *paradeisos*, using it not to refer to the wall itself but to the huge parks that Persian nobles loved to build and hunt in. This Greek word was used in the Septuagint translation of Genesis to refer to the Garden of Eden, and then Latin translations of the Bible used the Greek word in its Latinized form, *paradisus*. The Latin word was then borrowed into Old English and used to designate the Garden of Eden. In Middle English, the form of the word was influenced by its Old French equivalent, *paradis*, and it is from such Middle English forms as *paradis* that our Modern English word descends."

MEANING OF *TRADITION*

So much for *paradise*. What does *tradition* mean for us Catholics? In its formal and technical sense, the word has two distinct meanings. First, "Tradition" in the singular and with a capital T is one of the two founts of divine revelation, together with Holy Scripture: it can therefore not be dispensed with. Second, "traditions" in the plural and with a small t encompasses diverse customs prevalent in certain eras and areas of the Church: those are susceptible of changes.[2] In more general usage, "tradition" includes the holy thing handed by someone to another, and the act or process of transmitting. Over the past fifty years, within the Catholic Church, many have been led to interpret *tradition* as a hindrance, as something negative which would prevent the Holy Ghost from acting fully in every soul, in the Church and in the world. On the opposite side, a small minority has stood up in the name of traditions defended as a necessary guidance for authentic Catholic growth, for sanctification and evangelisation. The holy Gospels bear witness to the possible misuse of traditions. Thus, Our Blessed Lord strongly reproached the Pharisees who invoked a cultic precept from Moses to excuse themselves from supporting their elderly parents: "*You*

---

2    Cf. *Catechism of the Catholic Church* # 83: "Tradition is to be distinguished from the various theological, disciplinary, liturgical or devotional traditions, born in the local churches over time. These are the particular forms, adapted to different places and times, in which the great Tradition is expressed. In the light of Tradition, these traditions can be retained, modified or even abandoned under the guidance of the Church's Magisterium."

*make void the commandment of God, that you may keep your own tradition"* (Mk 7:9). Is Jesus condemning traditions? Not so. He is reminding the sect of the Pharisees that their custom was merely invented by men, so that it cannot be given precedence over the commandment given by God himself on Mount Sinai. In other words, not all that is handed down by men deserves retaining, especially not when clashing with God's revelation. Later on, the Lord Jesus *"spoke to the multitudes and to his disciples, Saying: The scribes and the Pharisees have sitten on the chair of Moses. All things therefore whatsoever they shall say to you, observe and do: but according to their works do ye not; for they say, and do not"* (Mt 23:1-3). The Lord commands them to observe the traditions handed down from Moses who received them from God. Observing such traditions means of course implementing them not perfunctorily or hypocritically, but with a sincere heart so as to honour God and one's neighbour in truth and charity. Our Lord did observe some traditions, such as using a cup of wine to celebrate Passover, which was not prescribed in the Torah but subsequently became a Jewish custom. Similarly, St Paul commanded the early Christians: *"Therefore, brethren, stand fast; and hold the traditions which you have learned, whether by word, or by our epistle"* (2 Thess 2:15). What is taught or ordered directly from the Lord and what is commanded by God's apostles must be upheld always. A wider consideration on Catholic Tradition would far exceed the scope of this little essay. Suffice it to point out that liturgical traditions command adherence and love inasmuch as they have successfully kept alive the faith of the Church from one generation of believers to the next. In the traditional form of holy Mass, the truths which Christ has revealed to us through his apostles[3] and which his Holy Ghost has detailed further through the magisterium of his Church[4] are expressed with clarity, displayed with beauty and taught with certainty. We list below such Eucharistic truths.

---

3   Cf. 1 Cor 11:23–29: "For I have received of the Lord that which also I delivered unto you, that the Lord Jesus, the same night in which he was betrayed, took bread. And giving thanks, broke, and said: Take ye, and eat: this is my body, which shall be delivered for you: this do for the commemoration of me. In like manner also the chalice, after he had supped, saying: This chalice is the new testament in my blood: this do ye, as often as you shall drink, for the commemoration of me. For as often as you shall eat this bread, and drink the chalice, you shall shew the death of the Lord, until he come. Therefore whosoever shall eat this bread, or drink the chalice of the Lord unworthily, shall be guilty of the body and of the blood of the Lord. But let a man prove himself: and so let him eat of that bread, and drink of the chalice. For he that eateth and drinketh unworthily, eateth and drinketh judgment to himself, not discerning the body of the Lord."
4   Cf. *Catechism of the Catholic Church* ##1322–1419.

## MAIN EUCHARISTIC TRUTHS[5]

1. Holy Mass is the unbloody re-enactment of the sacrifice of Christ on the Cross for the remission of sins, performed by the ordained priest acting *in persona Christi*.
2. Nothing is more pleasing to God and beneficial to souls than the diligent offering of the holy Sacrifice of the Mass, even daily.
3. The priest celebrant acts by virtue of the divine power to transubstantiate, forever embedded in his soul through the rite of priestly ordination.
4. Under the externals of bread and wine, Jesus Christ, true God and true Man, makes himself really, truly and substantially present.
5. By virtue of concomitance, Christ is present with his Body, Blood, Soul and divinity under the externals of bread.
6. By virtue of concomitance, Christ is present with his Body, Blood, Soul and divinity also under the externals of wine.
7. Christ's presence in the Holy Eucharist is supreme and unsurpassed on earth.
8. His Eucharistic presence lasts as long as the externals of bread and wine remain, even in very small quantities; even after holy Mass has ended.

---

5   Recent Church Magisterium upholds them as showed in modern catechisms and, among other texts, in Pope Paul VI's encyclical *Mysterium Fidei*; in Pope John-Paul II's encyclical *Ecclesia de Eucharistia*; and in Pope Benedict XVI's post-synodal exhortation *Sacramentum Caritatis*.

9. The congregation offers the divine Victim with and through the priest, and its members are brought in closer unity with each other to the extent in which they unite with Christ in faith and charity.

10. Active participation in holy Mass is union through faith and charity with Christ, Priest and Victim, perfectly achieved and exemplified by Our Blessed Lady as she stood at the foot of the Cross on Good Friday.

11. As reconciliation with God enables reconciliation among men, holy Mass is a fraternal meal only in dependence and as an effect of its being primarily a sacrifice offered to God.

12. Those fasting for one hour at least and in a state of grace can receive Holy Communion with due reverence and with thanksgiving.

13. Such communicants have their venial sins erased.

14. Receiving Holy Communion while in a state of mortal sin is a sacrilege and must be accused and absolved in Confession.

15. Attending holy Mass every Sunday and on major feasts is a commandment of the Church, unless exempt.

16. Receiving Holy Communion once a year at least is a commandment of the Church.

17. The sacrifice of the Mass is invisibly attended by the Blessed Virgin Mary, the holy angels and the saints.

18. The sacrifice of the Mass benefits those not physically present such as the holy

souls in Purgatory, all the faithful on earth, and obtains graces for the repentance of sinners and the conversion of all non-Catholics.

19. Living faith determines the amount of graces received at Holy Mass as mind and heart adhere to the invisible Eucharistic truths.

20. Since the human mind knows nothing but through the five bodily senses, and since knowledge is a condition for faith, liturgical words, gestures, melodies, architecture, vestments, furniture, perfumes, vessels and all such items must concur to express the Eucharistic truths as unambiguously and eloquently as possible.

Members of the faithful who unexpectedly stepped into the secret garden of holy traditions found their faith strengthened and nourished as never before. They realised this as a matter of experience, with no intention of judging fellow Catholics from other parishes. The newcomers were simply grateful to God, to holy Church and to the bishops and priests enabling access to these holy traditions for the benefits of any soul. For instance, they soon noticed how everyone genuflected to the tabernacle whenever walking across the central aisle as if, out the most sacred part of the building, some invisible beam projected up the main aisle at man's height, preventing upright wandering. Acquiring the habit of bending their knee towards the holy of holies every time they walked by unconsciously fortified their faith in the Real Presence of the Lord Jesus in the tabernacle. They candidly rejoiced, as evoked in the Psalm comparing souls to birds seeking rest around God's altars, *"How lovely are thy tabernacles, O Lord of host! My soul longeth and fainteth for the courts of the Lord. My heart and my flesh have rejoiced in the living God. For the sparrow hath found herself a house, and the turtle a nest for herself where she may lay her young ones: Thy altars, O Lord of hosts, my king and my God. Blessed are they that dwell in thy house, O Lord: they shall praise thee for ever and ever... For God loveth mercy and truth: the Lord will give grace and glory. He will not deprive of good things them that walk in innocence."*[6]

---

6  Psalm 84: 1–4, 11–12.

## *Conclusion*

---

# OPENING UP
# THE GARDEN OF
# HOLY TRADITIONS

**O**N WHAT EXTENT does the metaphor of holy traditions as a secret garden apply? First, why a garden, which refers to a place, whereas a tradition is a process? Second, why a *secret* garden, since the holy traditions of the Church are her shared patrimony and her public treasure, which seems to preclude secrecy?

We answer that a garden is the setting where the process of natural growth best occurs. The metaphor of holy traditions as a garden illustrates the fact that such traditions are precious goods which of their nature demand a separation from the world, as are the soil and plants cultivated within a walled garden, sheltered from cattle and strong winds. The prophet Isaiah used this metaphor to describe God's care for his people — God's cherished *vine* — and the divine chastisement for Israel's unfruitfulness.[1] Divine cultivation applies especially to the holy traditions as embodied and implemented in the Eucharistic Sacrifice, *"which is the fount and apex of the whole Christian life."*[2] The art of planting and nurturing seeds describes adequately two essential qualities of the holy traditions, namely, their gratuitous origin and their organic development. Unlike man-made artefacts, which come out of the skilled hands of craftsmen, plants are a gift from God through nature. The former are products made, whereas the latter are

---

1   My beloved had a vineyard on a hill in a fruitful place. And he fenced it in, and picked the stones out of it, and planted it with the choicest vines...
    And now I will shew you what I will do to my vineyard. I will take away the hedge thereof, and it shall be wasted: I will break down the wall thereof, and it shall be trodden down. And I will make it desolate: it shall not be pruned, and it shall not be digged: but briers and thorns shall come up: and I will command the clouds to rain no rain upon it. For the vineyard of the Lord of hosts is the house of Israel: and the man of Juda, his pleasant plant: and I looked that he should do judgment, and behold iniquity: and do justice, and behold a cry (Isaiah 5:1–2, 5–7).

2   As Vatican II defined in *Lumen Gentium* (Chapter 2, #11).

living things received. Admittedly, gardening tools are needed to tend, trim and stake
plants, while the soil may require fertilising
and irrigation, but none of these things *creates*
vegetal life: they merely support and enhance
it. Analogically, the holy traditions stem from
the supernatural seed of the Gospel planted
by Christ the divine "gardener."[3] They are
inspired by the Holy Ghost, Soul of the Church.
Holy Church faithfully tends them but cannot
invent or fabricate them the way an engineer
designs components or an artisan assembles
parts in a workshop. Even though Our Lord
spent thirty years in a carpenter's workshop
in Nazareth, a workshop (even more so a fac-
tory) fails to evoke the gift of life and organic
development the way a garden does.

Why then is the garden a *secret* one? Indeed,
the garden was not meant to be kept secret.
An accident caused its locking up. As illustrated in Burnett's novel, the garden of the
beloved mother was a place of restful toil
and of peaceful encounter where anyone who
sought was to be welcomed, guided and fed. If
such a garden has fallen into near oblivion, it
is because the father of the house, the paterfa-
milias, laden with sorrow, once buried the key.

---

3    John 20:15 "Jesus saith to her: Woman, why weepest
thou? whom seekest thou? She, thinking it was the gardener, saith to him: Sir, if thou hast taken him hence, tell
me where thou hast laid him, and I will take him away."

The garden was not meant to be concealed. At Misselthwaite Manor, very few remembered the garden of delights. But when the children providentially found access to it again, all rejoiced, and the wider estate benefitted from it. Similarly, the holy traditions of the Church are time-proven channels of divine grace to souls. Holy traditions don't belong in museums, attics or even private chapels but call for ubiquitous display and generous availability, as was the case in every village church up to the 1960s. It would seem that the sacramental collapse caused by the Covid-19 ordeal has led more faithful and converts, seeking spiritual assistance, to encounter the holy traditions once so familiar to Catholics in England. The same applies in many other countries all over the world. While this trend is still numerically marginal, it should be appreciated as a sign of supernatural growth and thus of hope for the Church universal.

Whereas any soul should seek shelter and healing in the liturgical garden, its shade is no cowardly refuge for the faint-hearted. On the contrary, it is meant as God's nursery to help souls mature into powerful witnesses of his truth and love throughout the world. What the heroine below stated about her encounter in the natural garden of her family home can be applied to any Christian soul raised in the supernatural garden of the traditional liturgy: *"Then came that voice, about the hour of noon: in summer time, in my father's garden...."* These are the authentic words[4] of St Joan of Arc (1412–1431) according to the transcripts of her trial. In a quiet setting of natural beauty, as the Angelus rang at the nearby village church, the humble shepherdess of Domremy was visited by the ambassadors of the heavenly Father and sent on a mission that changed the course of history.[5] Similarly, if less spectacularly, any soul nurtured in the garden of the traditional liturgy is summoned with love by God Almighty through his ministers and sent on the most momentous of journeys — the conversion of the world for the glory of God and the salvation of men: *"Ite, missa est!"*[6] Evangelisation stems

---

4 French original : "Puis vint cette voix, Environ l'heure de midi, Au temps de l'été, Dans le jardin de mon père." François Cheng of the *Académie Française* called these four lines a quatrain, possibly the purest in the French language, and one that "all French-speakers should learn by heart." Furthermore, poet and playwright Jean Cocteau (1889–1963) called St. Joan of Arc "our greatest writer."
5 If one sought a musical setting while meditating on this event, perhaps Ralph Vaughan Williams' *Fantasia on "Greensleeves"* (1934) could be suggested. The much-loved English piece aptly evokes the quiet, then the surprise, and finally the sending and the promise of peace sacrificially secured.
6 "Go, the Mass is ended!" These are the conclusive words of Holy Mass before the Final Blessing and Last Gospel, also interpreted as "marching orders" for the faithful.

from contemplation deeply rooted in liturgical tradition. Ultimately, the entire world is to be turned into "Our Father's Garden." The "secret" of salvation is meant to be shared with all men, as Our Blessed Lord himself commanded: *"That which I tell you in the dark, speak ye in the light: and that which you hear in the ear, preach ye upon the housetops"* (Matthew 10:27).[7]

We introduced our reflexion using a text of fiction for children, *The Secret Garden*, written by non-Catholic author Frances Hodgson Burnett. It seems fitting to end with another description of a garden, but of a genuine one this time rather than imagined; one given by a heroic Catholic and a confessor of the faith, the Venerable Stefan Wyszyński[8] who, already Cardinal and Archbishop Primate of Poland, was imprisoned for over three years by the Communists. The following extract from his prison diary focuses on the neglected garden outside the insalubrious former friary where he was detained, fenced off from the world but close to God.[9]

---

7  Needless to say, this command to evangelise is addressed to all Catholics, whichever liturgical rite they attend.
8  His beatification by Pope Francis was postponed until autumn 2021 due to Covid-19.
9  *A Freedom Within, The Prison Notes of Stefan, Cardinal Wyszyński*, published by Aid to the Church in Need, 1982, England, p.94.

The garden was our great delight. All winter long the two of us were a brigade battling the snow that blocked the paths. This work consumed much of our energy. We fed the birds in 'cafeterias' in the cedars and on the roof of the porch. Spring was delightful: the snowdrops amazed us with their power as they broke through the hard, icy surfaces; next, liverworts and periwinkles adorned the lawn that had looked like a rubbish heap in the fall. When the yellow sow this-tle and the fruit trees blossomed, the sight was unforgettable. We fell in love with the starlings, whose motherly concerns and community lessons, but most especially the gluttony of the young, amazed us. All this enthusiasm for eating, so much plead-ing in the little gaping beaks, such great effort in providing can all serve as subject for meditation for many hours. How much one can see in a detached segment of the world, when one is forced to look only short range — I first realised in Stoczek. If such a tiny piece of ground is so rich in life, what can be said of the whole earth?

## ABOUT THE AUTHOR

FR ARMAND DE MALLERAY, FSSP holds a Master's Degree in Modern Literature from the University of The Sorbonne in Paris. Ordained a priest and first assigned in England in 2001, he has been the editor of the quarterly magazine *Dowry* since 2008 and is the author of theological essays, of fiction and of art commentaries. He regularly preaches retreats to the clergy and the laity, and to young members of the *Juventutem* youth movement of which he has been the general chaplain since 2004. Since 2015, he is rector of St Mary's Shrine Church in the Archdiocese of Liverpool, England.

## WORKS BY THE SAME AUTHOR

*Meditations on the Stabat Mater*, spirituality (London, UK: Catholic Truth Society, 2022)

*Ego Eimi: It is I — Falling in Eucharistic Love*, essay (Nashua, NH: Sophia Institute Press, 2022)

*Near Missed Masses*, fiction (Waterloo, ON: Arouca Press, 2021)

*X-Ray of the Priest in a Field Hospital*, essay (Waterloo, ON: Arouca Press, 2020)

*Italian Renaissance, Art for Souls*, art commentary; CD-ROM (Versailles, France: Rejoyce, 2004)

*Caravage, l'art pour l'âme*, art commentary; CD-ROM (Versailles, France: Rejoyce, 2001)

*La Tour, l'art pour l'âme*, art commentary; CD-ROM (Versailles, France: Rejoyce, 2000)